The Roman Pantheon: The History and Legac

By Charles River Editors

Alessio Nastro Siniscalchi's picture of the Pantheon

About Charles River Editors

Charles River Editors provides superior editing and original writing services across the digital publishing industry, with the expertise to create digital content for publishers across a vast range of subject matter. In addition to providing original digital content for third party publishers, we also republish civilization's greatest literary works, bringing them to new generations of readers via ebooks.

Sign up here to receive updates about free books as we publish them, and visit Our Kindle Author Page to browse today's free promotions and our most recently published Kindle titles.

Introduction

Jean-Pol Grandmont's picture of the Pantheon

The Roman Pantheon

"Of the whole mighty fabric of his productions, more lasting than himself, whereby man establishes the identity of his species in all ages, there is none more principal stone than the Pantheon of Rome." – R.H. Busk, 19th century Pantheon scholar

From as early as the 3rd century BCE, the Romans were prodigious monument builders, so much so that the memory of the great Roman Republic and the Roman Empire continues to exist within a cityscape of stone. Rome's public spaces were filled with statues, arches, temples, and many other varieties of monumental images, and each of these structures had its own civic or religious function. At the same time, most were embedded with stories, messages, and symbolism so that they also tended to function as propaganda. These monuments allowed the leading citizens of Rome, especially its emperors, to sculpt their own self-image and embed themselves and their most memorable deeds into the very structure of the Roman city.

As the most completely preserved building of the Imperial Roman capital, the Pantheon represents the peak of Imperial monument building at Rome. It is no coincidence that the Pantheon was built during the zenith of the Roman empire's power and wealth; as with most civilizations, this period of exceptional commercial and political activity was symbolized by large-scale building. In this respect, the Pantheon is a visual symbol of the greatness of the Roman Empire, and as such, it captivates all who have been privileged enough to behold it. Michelangelo declared the building to be of "angelic and not human design," while Goethe claimed to be "overwhelmed with admiration" for the structure.

While the sublime nature of the Pantheon's design has always been readily apparent, no one has ever been able to figure out exactly what the structure was supposed to mean or even how it was built. Stepping into the Pantheon's soaring, curved interior is itself enough to make anyone feel insignificant by comparison, and this feeling is only reinforced by the elusiveness of its meaning and design. In a sense, however, the fact that the Pantheon seems doomed to be forever shrouded in mystery only serves to enhance its captivating beauty.

The Roman Pantheon: The History and Legacy of Rome's Famous Landmark chronicles the construction of the Pantheon and its long history as one of Rome's best preserved sites. Along with pictures of important people, places, and events, you will learn about the Pantheon like never before, in no time at all.

The Roman Pantheon: The History and Legacy of Rome's Famous Landmark
About Charles River Editors
Introduction
   Chapter 1: The Original Pantheon
   Chapter 2: Hadrian and the Pantheon
   Chapter 3: The Meaning of Hadrian's Pantheon
   Chapter 4: The Pantheon after Hadrian
   Online Resources
   Bibliography

Chapter 1: The Original Pantheon

"I have just seen the Pantheon, which I take to be the finest and most perfect work of ancient Times that Rome, and after that, I need not say, that the World, has to boast. One is astonished to hear that Agrippa planned, designed, founded, and perfected the Pantheon. Less than Emperor has the Honour of having begun and finished the greatest building of the World. A private Roman was able to leave behind him a monument of Taste and of Experience which shames the Pride of Kings. The Term sounds oddly; but we know that Agrippa was considerable enough by the near Relation in which he stood to Augustus, and, as the merit of his peculiar Virtues, to have Coins struck to him; an Honour allowed in that time only to the Emperor, Empress, and their adopted Children." – Anonymous visitor in the 18th century

Marcus Vipsanius Agrippa, friend and son-in-law of Augustus and architect of many of the marble structures about which Augustus was known to boast,[1] began construction on the first building that was to be called the Roman Pantheon in 27 BCE. Not much remains of the original structure, but from what little evidence archaeologists have been able to gather, Agrippa's Pantheon seems to have been a building of the ordinary classical temple type. The first Pantheon was likely a rectangular structure with a gabled roof, supported on all sides by a colonnade. The foundation of an early structure built on the site of the existing Pantheon, which scholars suspect belonged to Agrippa's building, is rectangular and measures 43.76 meters wide by 19.82 meters long. The travertine foundations suggest that the original Pantheon was a decastyle temple with 10 columns on each of its long sides. The façade of Agrippa's Pantheon faced to the south; this southern front of the original temple opened a large round space which was enclosed by a non-supporting edge. The pavement of the space was not horizontal; its pavonazzetto[2] marble slabs sloped downwards towards the circumference of the slightly conical open circle which was most likely the site of the first temple's altar.

---

[1] Augustus famously boasted that he found Rome a city of brick and left it a city of marble (Suet. *Aug.* 29). During his lengthy reign, Augustus was determined to renovate the city of Rome so that its buildings matched the grandeur of his empire. It was in no small part thanks to Agrippa that Augustus was able to achieve this vision. As a Roman aedile (one of his many titles), Agrippa was responsible for Rome's buildings and festivals. Agrippa restored and built Rome's aqueducts, enlarged and cleansed the Cloaca Maxima, and constructed a great number of gardens, porticos, baths, and other civic structures.
[2] One of the many varieties of Carrara marble, pavonazzetto marble is distinguished by its irregular veins of dark red, as well as its blueish and yellow tints. Its name derives from the Italian word for peacock (*pavone*).

An ancient bust of Agrippa

An ancient statue of Augustus

Archaeologists continue to debate the exact internal arrangement of the initial structure. According to the Roman naturalist Pliny the Elder, the only Roman author who may have looked directly upon the original Pantheon, Agrippa's Pantheon was decorated with a colossal stature of Venus which was adorned with a pearl that once belonged to Cleopatra.[3] According to Pliny, the

---

[3] Pliny recounts the story of Cleopatra's pearls at length: "The last of the Egyptian queens," he says, "owned the two largest pearls of all time, left to her by oriental kings. When Antony was stuffing himself daily with rare foods, she proudly and impertinently, like the royal harlot that she was, sneered at his attempts at luxury and extravagance. When he asked her what could be added in the way of sumptuousness she replied that she would use up 10,000,000 sesterces at one dinner. Antony was eager to learn about it but didn't think it could be done. So they made a bet, and on the next day when the bet was to be decided, she set before Antony a dinner that under other circumstances would have been a magnificent one but was an everyday affair for Antony. She did this so that the day should not be entirely wasted. Antony laughed at her and asked for the reckoning. But she said that this was merely a preliminary and assured him that the real banquet would use up the estimated sum and

structure also featured statues of Julius Caesar and Mars, the Roman god of war and the god from whom Julius Caesar claimed to have descended. There may have also been statues of Augustus and Marcus Agrippa himself. The temple was further embellished with caryatids[4] and figures on the angles of the pediment.

Since many of these sculptures were of Roman citizens, it is clear that Agrippa's Pantheon must have had a function that was civic as well as religious, but that precise function is unknown.[5] In fact, no one has any idea what Agrippa's structure was originally called. All that Roman historians have thus far been able to establish is that the nickname "Pantheon" was not applied to the building until at least a few years after its construction. According to the Roman historian Cassius Dio, the building was called the Pantheon "perhaps because it received among the images which decorated it the statues of many gods, including Mars and Venus." Dio, however, was skeptical of this explanation and proposed his own alternative: "My own opinion of the name is that, because of its vaulted roof, it resembles the heavens."

Not long after construction on the first Pantheon had been complete, Rome was devastated by an earthquake. The 19 foot walls of the Pantheon, which were perforated with all three stages of chambers that ran completely around the building to keep the structure dry and earthquake proof, remained unscathed, but there are ancient reports that the quake shook the scepter from the hand of the statue of Augustus. During the reign of Titus (79-81 CE), however, the Pantheon was entirely destroyed by a great fire.[6]

---

that she would consume the half-million dollar dinner all by herself. Then she ordered the dessert to be served. According to instructions, the servants placed but one dish before her, containing vinegar whose acidity and strength dissolves pearls into slush. She was at the time wearing in her ears that remarkable and truly unique work of nature known as pearls. So while Antony was wondering what in the world she was going to do, she took one pearl from her ear, plunged it into the vinegar, and when it was dissolved, swallowed it. Lucius Plancus, who was refereeing the bet, put his hand on the other pearl as she was preparing to dissolve it in like manner and declared Antony the loser." It was, in fact, this second pearl that was worn by the Venus of Agrippa's Pantheon.

[4] A carytid is a sculpted female figure that serves as an architectural support in the place of a column or a pillar; she supports an entablature on her head.

[5] Some scholars have proposed that Agrippa's Pantheon was built as a monument of Augustus' victory over Marc Anthony in the naval battle at Actium.

[6] That a granite building could be utterly destroyed by fire has been yet another source of confusion for scholars of the Pantheon. In the words of one: "In all these reports of fires, however, there is one thing which I fail to understand, and that is how fire could have attacked, injured, or altogether destroyed edifices built of marble and bronze, without a particle of timber or other combustible material. Take, for example, the Pantheon of Agrippa, which ancient writers assert was twice burnt...there is not an atom of it capable of catching fire; not even Frenc petroleurs could do it the slightest harm."

Ancient bust of Titus

Archaeological excavations have revealed traces of an intermediate pavement above Agrippa's, and it has been established that this pavement belonged to a structure created by the emperor Domitian (81-96 CE) as an attempted restoration of the first Pantheon not long after the first building was destroyed.

Approximately 30 years later, during the reign of the emperor Trajan (98-117 CE), the building burned down for the second time after being struck by a bolt of lightning. Trajan did not have time to rebuild the Pantheon - he died abruptly in August of 117 - but Trajan's sudden death provided his successor, Publius Aelius Hadrianus (117-138), then the governor of Syria, with the lucrative opportunity to rebuild on the site of the original Pantheon.

An ancient bust of Trajan

Chapter 2: Hadrian and the Pantheon

An ancient bust of Hadrian

"One night (I was eleven years old at the time) [my great uncle] came and shook me from my sleep and announced, with the same grumbling laconism that he would have employed to predict a good harvest to his tenants, that I should rule the world." – Hadrian

"A brazen Gate opens to admit one from the Portico into the Temple, and the Door-Case is one entire Piece of Marble; it is fifty Feet in Height, and nearly half as much in Breadth. What a Block must it have been to furnish it! what a Taske to attempt cutting it! what Art to succeed!

...The round Figure of this Temple, from which it is at present called the Rotunda, gives it a very singular, and at the same Time a very noble Look; and there is something very solemn and awful in the enlightening of it, which is all done from a large Opening in the Crown of the Vault; for there are no Windows. This Opening, in Spite of all Contrivances, will let in Wet in bad Weather, but 'tis of little Consequence, nothing that can be injured is placed immediately under it..."[7] – Anonymous visitor in the 18th century

The builder-emperor (and empire-builder) Hadrian, the Pantheon and the cultural context of the early 2nd century are all inexorably interwoven. Hadrian was born in 76 in Roman Spain to an established colonial family during the reign of the emperor Vespasian, and by nearly all accounts Hadrian became a deeply cultivated man well-versed in Greek (as was expected of a Roman aristocrat). Though he was said to be a rather restless and difficult person, he nevertheless bore his many responsibilities well, as he was exceptionally intelligent and accomplished in a number of different activities. In addition to his administrative and military feats, Hadrian was also a poet, a painter, and an architect.

Perhaps most significantly (at least as far as the Pantheon is concerned), the Greek sophist Philostratus noted that Hadrian was an avid Pythagorean. Indeed, it would be a combination of Hadrian's proclivity towards Pythagoreanism and his affinity for astronomy that would eventually shape his design of the Pantheon.

According to Cassius Dio, Hadrian was constantly motivated by extraordinary dreams, as well as by his impassioned interests in astrology, divination, and magic, not to mention by his secondary interests in architecture, literature, and painting. Hadrian was known to consult many astrologers (his own uncle was a master of astrology), and Hadrian himself was indeed so proficient in astrology that he kept astrological journals right up until the hour of his death. He also consulted oracles and was quite serious about heeding their omens and prophecies, especially those that related to his ascent to power and fame. The great emperor may have even

---

[7] The visitor continues at length, seemingly desperate to convey the beauty of the Pantheon to his reader. He tells of structures described in this section with more clarity and concision; however, his words add wonderful, richly-textured detail to the aforementioned description, and as such they bear repeating here: "[T]he Walls [of the Pantheon] are plain; but though there are no Ornaments that project there, there are Representations of the Orders of Architecture inlaid in the Marble. They call this part the Tambour or Drum of the building. From the Top of this Tambour, springs the Vault. This makes the upper Half of the Temple, as the Pillars and Tambour do the lower Half. This is divided into quadrangular Compartments hollowed, and the Ribs which project between them, terminate in the Round of the Opening at Top; between each of the Altars round the Sides, that go beyond the Circle, there are others that stand within it. The lesser ones have the Pillars Intablature, and the Frontispiece of Porphyry, the antique yellow, and others are rich Marbles; and their flat parts are encrusted with Marble...the Floor of the Pantheon is paved in the most pompous Manner with Marble, not with the common, but the most costly Kinds. In the Center is a vast round Slab of Porphyry, which has a Hole through it, to let down the Water from the Opening at Top. The great Altar stands opposite to the Gate of the Temple, and there are on each Side three lesser, taking up all the Space from the great one to the Door, at regular Distances. All these are placed in hollowed Spaces, running beyond the line of the general Circle; and they make so many Chapels. At the Entrance of each there is, on either Side, a noble Pillar and Pilasters of antique a yellow Marble; they are of the Corinthian Order fluted, and the Capitals and Base are of white Marble; they support the great Intablature that goes round."

wrote some prophecies himself. Hadrian made sure to keep a number of astrologers, geometricians, and astrologers within his circle of friends, though of course he was himself expertly proficient in geometry, arithmetic, painting, and letters. Among Hadrian's most prized possessions was a primary Pythagorean text.

Hadrian believed in the immortality of the soul and that the universe was regulated entirely by laws of harmony and arithmetic. Like all good Pythagoreans, Hadrian also believed that every heavenly body was spherical in shape and that these shapes moved around a celestial fire. The Pythagoreans, Hadrian among them, placed an unusual importance upon the significance of numbers. For the Pythagoreans, the abstract concept of number was determined by the arrangement of points in a given form; thus, there existed within Pythagorean belief a diverse body of schemes that attached a secondary meaning to each number.

In the 1st century BCE, long before Hadrian would become a convert, Pythagoreanism had merged with Platonism and enjoyed a resurgence in popularity. During this period, Pythagoreanism came also to be associated with the pseudo-sciences, especially astrology, divination, and the interpretation of dreams. For centuries, adherents to Pythagoreanism would maintain an interest in new astronomical developments, and in the years leading up to Hadrian's rise to power, this interest came to shape an imaginary cosmology connected with the idea of the soul's immortality. Indeed, it was this imaginary cosmology that shaped much of Hadrian's own belief system.

As the Pythagoreans were developing their notion of cosmic order and universal harmony, educated Romans were beginning to develop a heightened interest in astrology. Some Roman emperors - especially those who, like Hadrian, spent time in the East - began to represent themselves as the immortal sun of the heavens. In the cosmic heaven, these emperors became deified supreme beings, and as such, the deified emperor-god assumed the role of cosmocrater, tasked with setting the lower planets in motion and directing the order of the world. Several Roman emperors prior to Hadrian represented themselves as the sun god, and the Roman world was full of images of these emperors portrayed with rays emanated from their heads as they sat in Apollo's horse-driven chariot.[8] Hadrian himself is known to have been represented in the four-horse chariot of the sun god.

Astrological forecasts were also of the utmost importance to the rulers of Rome. The Roman historian Suetonius mentions at great length both the horoscope of Hadrian's father and the famed horoscope of Hadrian himself. According to Suetonius, the horoscope of Hadrian's father predicted the birth of an illustrious son who would be subject to the influence of the moon. Hadrian's own horoscope (which would become another key element in Hadrian's design of the

---

[8] Hadrian may have surpassed even Nero in his apotheosis. Some scholars hypothesize that the ceiling of Hadrian's Villa at Tivoli was decorated with the globe of the firmament surrounded by the belt of the zodiac. Their hypothesis is supported by the two rotundas found at Tivoli.

Pantheon) began by expounding upon Hadrian's imperial destiny. In Hadrian's horoscope, the position of the moon and the sun were calculated in relation to the position of the other planets. Since these two major celestial luminaries were "attended" equally by the five other planets, they both looked to be at an equally critical point where they were attended by every other planet. The subsequent astrological conjecture was that the person who was born under this configuration – Hadrian - was destined to one day become the ruler of the world. Hadrian's horoscope then went on to predict his education and his wisdom, his childlessness, and, ultimately, his death from illness. Most appropriately, Hadrian's horoscope had unmistakably Pythagorean undertones, as its contents implied that the sun and the moon[9] would be the guarantors of Hadrian's immortality.

Given this horoscope as part of his background, it is perhaps not surprising that Hadrian was a man of insatiable ambition. Throughout the course of his life, Hadrian was consumed by the desire to surpass everyone in everything. Hadrian allowed the Athenians to build an altar to him, and throughout Asia, he consecrated a number of temples to himself. When the Greeks deified him, it was at his own request. Oracles were given through him, and Hadrian routinely ridiculed and humiliated both professors and philosophers in order to demonstrate that he was superior to them. He authored and distributed his own autobiography so that he could ensure his reputation throughout the entire Roman world. He named a number of cities and countless aqueducts after himself. In one location where he supposedly killed a bear singlehandedly, he immediately consecrated it as "Hadrianotherae." When he at last defeated Jerusalem, he dubbed the vanquished city "Aelia" after his own praenomen. He was all but consumed by his ardent hatred for all those who aspired to succeed him, so much so that he compelled many of these would-be successors to kill themselves.

Given that he was a man of such fierce ambition, there is not a single one of Hadrian's biographers who did not suspect foul play in Hadrian's succession of Trajan. Since Trajan had died suddenly without a legal successor, Plotina, wife of Trajan and mistress to Hadrian's guardian Publius Attianus, used her own considerable influence to win Hadrian the empire. Though the Senate was the only Roman body that was authorized to confer rule upon an emperor, it never formally acknowledged Hadrian's claim to power; instead, Hadrian cleverly managed to assume power without returning to Rome, sending a carefully worded letter to the Senate in which he claimed that his troops had made him emperor by acclamation. Rome could

---

[9] For the entirety of his life, Hadrian thus remained devoted to the sun and the moon. This devotion is well reflected in the importance he placed upon his own birthday. According to Cassius Dio, Hadrian celebrated his birthday by staging grand spectacles which were free to attend for all the Roman people. In these spectacles, it was not unusual for two hundred lions to be killed at once. Spartianus goes on to describe the celebratory gladiator combats fought in honor of Hadrian's birthday—these sometimes lasted for six days! Hadrian's birthday was marked by the slaughter of one thousand wild beasts. On every other day of the year, Hadrian refused to allow circus games at Rome; however, he made an exception for his birthday. On his last birthday, Hadrian experienced two premonitions of his death: his toga falling down without reason, and a mysterious wailing sound which emanated from the Roman Senate.

not be without an emperor, and thus, Hadrian, with the alleged support of his army, was the logical choice to be the de facto emperor in this unusual situation. The Senate did not make an official objection to Hadrian's claim, and so Hadrian succeeded in becoming the emperor of Rome.

Hadrian remained in Syria for almost a year before finally returning to Rome in 117. He ordered the Roman people to annually celebrate the 9th of August, the day he received the news of Trajan's death, as a holiday. These celebrations were meant to mark the day upon which the prophecy about Hadrian's destiny had come true, and of course, the celebration would have also served to remind the people of Rome that Hadrian's destiny had been sanctioned by Apollo himself.

Perhaps unsurprisingly, Hadrian had quickly come to be hated by the Roman people, and when he finally returned to the city as the new emperor, he was greeted with overwhelming hostility. Shortly after arriving, a group of men made an attempt on Hadrian's life, and they failed only because Hadrian was able to evade them. At least four of these men were of consular rank, and when Hadrian put them to death, he only made himself more unpopular.

At this point, it became clear to Hadrian that he needed to do everything within his power to augment his popularity and reconcile the Roman people to his reign, and he implemented a number of measures to guarantee support for his rule. These steps included a remission of debts, providing assistance to public officials, making special allowances for senators, setting aside appropriations for those with children, and making sizable donations to a great number of individuals and causes alike.

It was also during this bid for popularity that Hadrian began to design the Pantheon, a hyper-visible symbol of his imperial power and majesty. Hadrian left Rome for an extended trip to Greece and the East that lasted until 127, so it can be assumed that he designed the Pantheon when he was at Rome in 118-19, and that the building was constructed during the seven years he was absent from Rome. When Hadrian finally returned to Rome in 127, the building was dedicated. This dating is suggested by the testimony of the historian Spartianus and confirmed by archaeological evidence. The bricks used in various parts of the monument bear stamps (*bolle*) of the time of Hadrian, and moreover, these bricks are of the particular composition used in Rome from 115-127. Some bricks used in the construction of the Pantheon were even embossed with the name of Julia Sabina, Hadrian's Empress.[10] The architect of the Pantheon is unknown,[11] but the building is fundamentally Hadrian's.

In all respects, the Pantheon was remarkable for its size, construction, design, and function.[12]

---

[10] According to Cassius Dio, these bricks supported a bench on which Hadrian sat in the Pantheon to administer justice.
[11] Hadrian's name has in fact been proposed as the architect behind the Pantheon, but this is at best unlikely.
[12] Unlike any of the other structures built by Hadrian, the Pantheon was both a place of personal worship and a place

Hadrian's Pantheon was approached by five marble steps, which elevated the structure from the forecourt, and an octastyle porch (*pronaos*) of Corinthian columns supported the Pantheon's gabled roof with an unusually high triangular pediment. This *pronaos* led to a barrel-vaulted entrance way, which featured a set of huge bronze double doors (the earliest known large examples of this type). A separate rectangular intermediate block as high as the entire building and as wide as the porch led into the Pantheon's rotunda, a third geometric area which was the primary space of the temple. Defined by brick and concrete structural elements and resting on a foundation of concrete that contains large travertine fragments, this third space forms a large circular ring corresponding in diameter and circumference with the formerly open paved space of Agrippa. This heart of Hadrian's structure is obviously new, as it was not built on the foundations of any preexisting building.

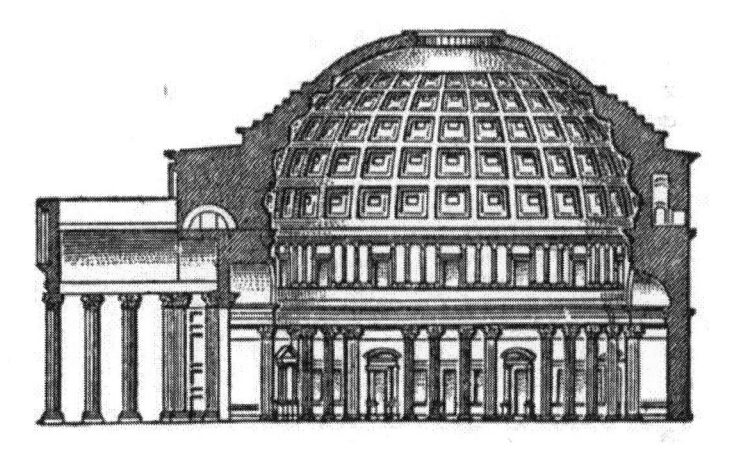

A model layout of the Pantheon

---

where Hadrian could hold court as emperor.

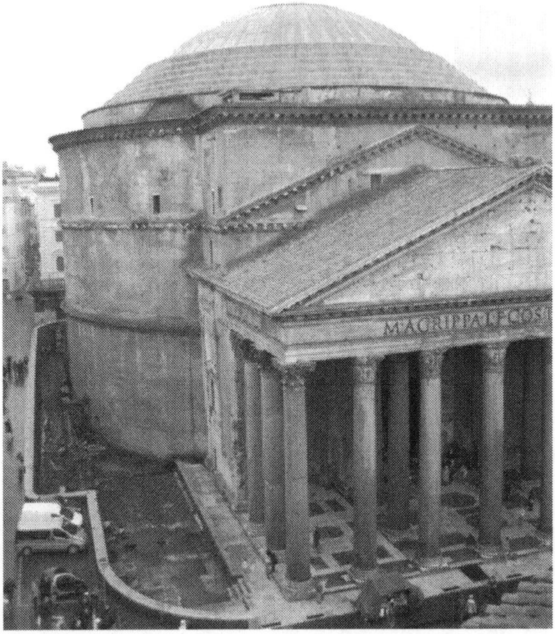
M·AGRIPPA·L·F·COS

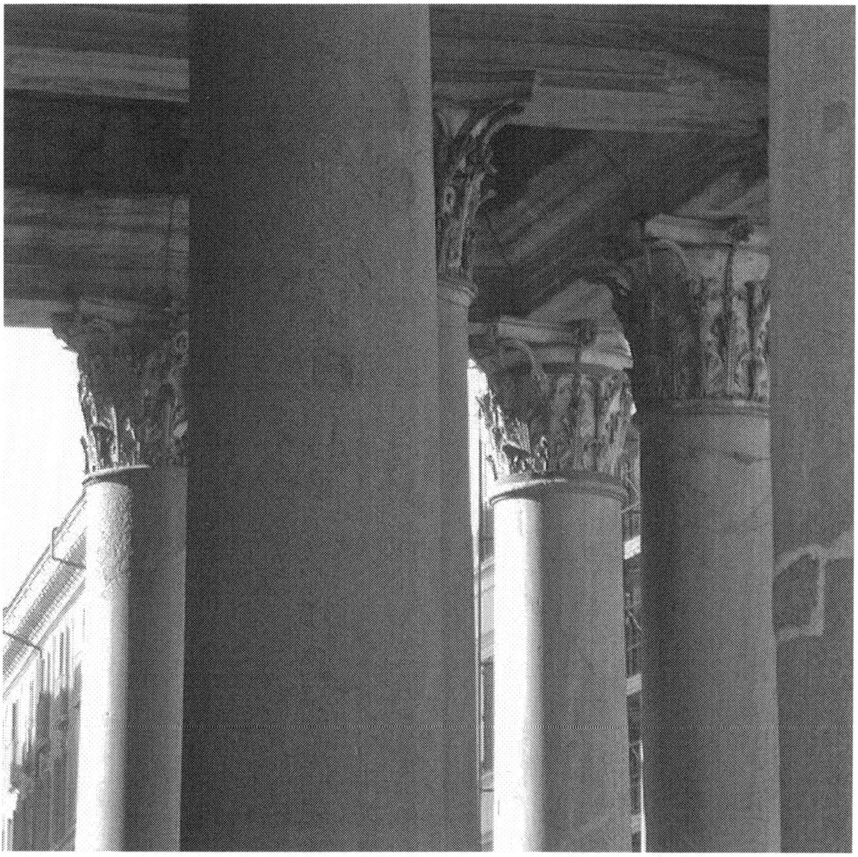

Pictures of some of the columns

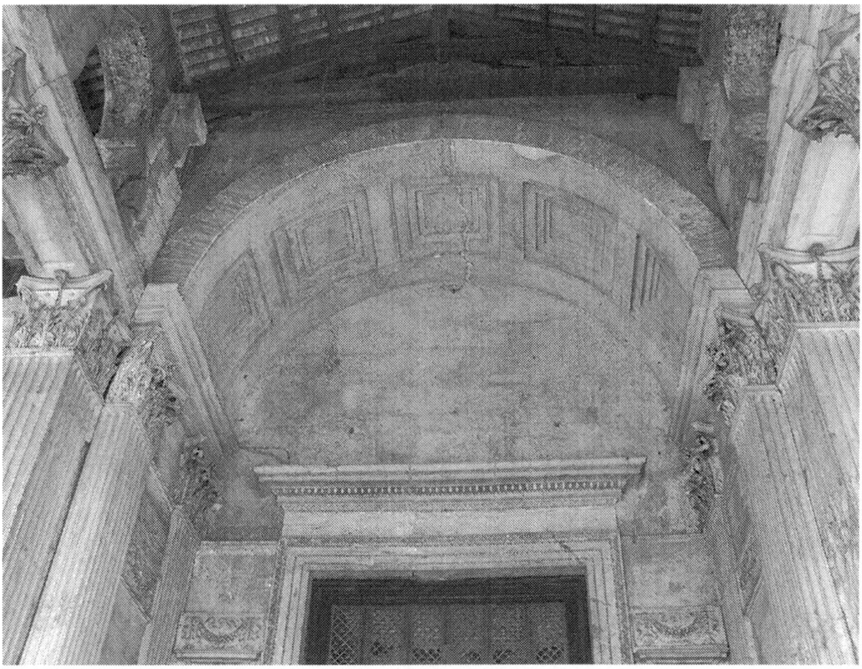

Pictures of the entrance way

Hadrian's Pantheon was at this point the most original temple the Roman world had ever known, for there had been no other temple designed that combined a pedimented porch with a circular construction. Some archaeologists have suggested that the Pantheon's *pronaos* is unrelated to its rotunda, and among them, a few suggest that Hadrian's temple may have incorporated the remaining parts of Agrippa's temple since the dimensions of the *pronaos* correspond roughly with those of the entire foundations of Agrippa's temple. The archaeological evidence, however, suggests that the entire structure, including the front porch, intermediate block, and rotunda, were all built at once by Hadrian.

As far as construction was concerned, the new temple had nothing to do with the old. This break in constructional continuity is underscored by the way in which Hadrian reversed the orientation of the temple. Hadrian's structure - oriented to the four cardinal directions - faced north (the only available space for a forecourt and altar), while Agrippa's structure had faced south.

The main segment of Hadrian's Pantheon was a circular building that was made of concrete and faced with brick. A great cylinder rose up from its circular foundation to support the largest domed rotunda ever built. This dome of the Pantheon, which spans an incredible 43.4 meters, was not matched for well over a millennium. It represents a culmination of the Roman architectural revolution brought to fruition during the course of the 1st century CE in large part due to the adoption of high quality concrete,[13] which was well-suited to the construction of curvilinear architectural forms. Indeed, the dome of Hadrian's Pantheon was so technologically advanced that it was not able to be significantly surpassed until the modern era began to use steel and reinforced concrete as building materials.

---

[13] Previously, buildings had been constructed with simple lime mortar. Lime mortar is produced by adding water to a mixture of quicklime and sand. The mixture sets when all the water has evaporated into the atmosphere or absorbed into the surrounding masonry. Roman "pozzolana" sets by combining chemically with water in the same way as modern Portland cement. Unlike lime mortar, pozzolana does not need to dry out—it's "hydraulic" in the sense that it will set even when immersed in water. Large batches of pozzolana curves relatively rapidly, even in damp conditions. The early compressive strength of pozzolana cement is also far superior to that of lime mortar. Given these properties, pozzolana was well-suited for use in constructing the massive primary structural elements of large buildings.

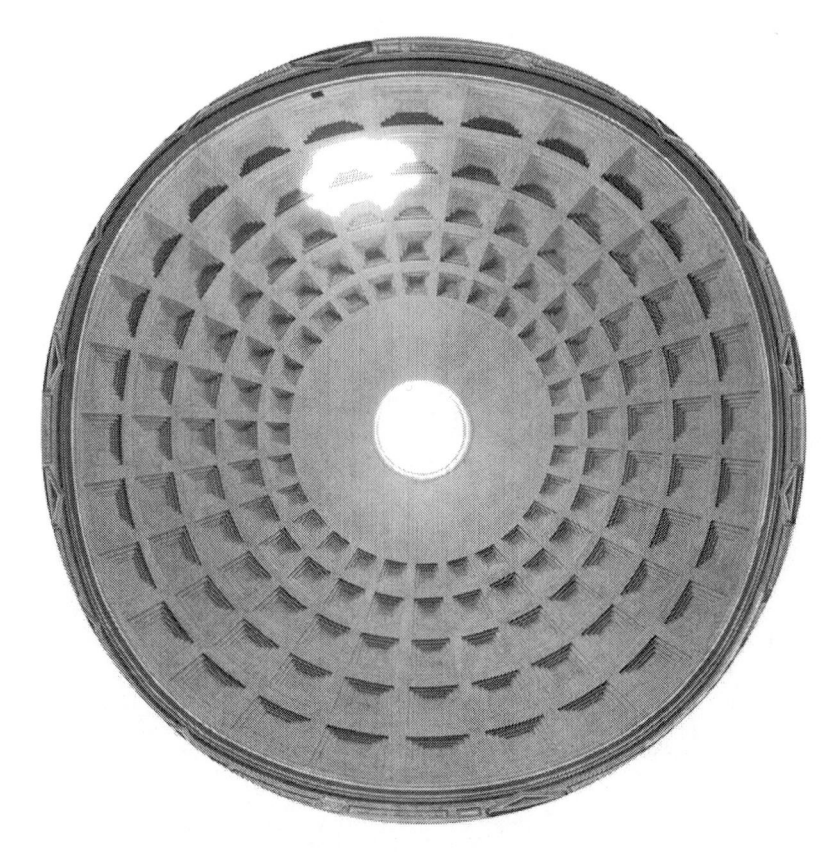

An interior view of the rotunda dome

Giovanni Paolo Panini's 18th century painting of the interior

Even to modern architects, the dome of the Pantheon remains something of an enigma. There is no evidence of brick arch supports inside the dome (expect in its lowest part), so the exact way in which Roman builders constructed the Pantheon's dome has never been determined. Nevertheless, architects have identified the two factors essential to its success: the excellent quality of the mortar used in its concrete and the careful selection and grading of the aggregate material.[14] Additionally, the uppermost third of the walls' drums (as seen from the outside),

---

[14] The material used in the Pantheon's aggregate ranges from heavy basalt in the building's foundations and the lower parts of its walls to brick and tufa in the middle parts of the structure. Towards the center of the vault, the lightest pumice was used as aggregate.

which coincides with the lower part of the dome (as seen from the inside), helps to contain the thrust with internal brick arches. Brick arches and piers set above one another inside the 6 meter thick walls help to strengthen the drum itself. The Pantheon's rotunda was equal in height and radius to the cylinder below.[15]

The body of the Pantheon thus consisted of a revolutionary immense circular space. Its interior was built with a controlling geometry based on a perfect central axis. Its horizontally and vertically aligned coffers were marked off by coffers which were aligned horizontally and vertically over the sloping surface of the dome, and these culminated in an oculus of unprecedented dimension. This oculus was centrally located over the interior space and poised over the central circle in the pavement.

---

[15] Demontius has suggested, since the present form of the Pantheon is nearly equal in its height and its width, that it formerly had another member which would have extended to a depth of thirteen palms below, and in place, the present pavement, and ranging on a level with the base of the external walls. According to Demontius, this would have contained altars dedicated to "the infernal deities," which would have been reached by a circular flight of steps. There would have been seven sunken cella (chapels) would have held altars to the celestial gods, and the spaces between would have help chapels to the celestial gods. The temple would therefore have celebrated all the various ideas under which the Deity was worshipped—it would have reduced the many Roman deities back to one.

Pictures of the oculus in the middle of the dome

The space of the Pantheon's rotunda was illuminated only by the light that pours through this eight meter oculus opening cut into the center of the dome.[16] This singular source of light for the entire building was originally crowned with an elaborate bronze cornice, which was likely also gilded. 19th century art historians who devoted their lives to the study of the Pantheon boast of how they had mounted its "190 ill-conditioned steps, and gazed down upon its vast area through the 'eye' of the summit. Standing nearly in the centre of the building, it is a view which may be termed with literal accuracy 'awful' as you perceive the surface on which you stand trending away from under you, an abyss spreading far away on every side; you might almost fancy yourself standing on a cloud 'in the third heaven.'" Located around the central aperture of the dome was an oak-leaf crown of gilded metal. The interior walls of the Pantheon were lined with colored marble and marked by seven deep recesses, screened by moderately sized columns—these gave scale to the immensity of the Pantheon's rotunda.

---

[16] Given both the spectacular effect this created in the Pantheon's interior and the Pantheon's relatively plain exterior, scholars have suggested that the Pantheon was one of the first great buildings of antiquity designed to favor the interior rather than the exterior.

A picture of the dome from a distance

Naturally, the decorations inside the Pantheon were extraordinarily elaborate. The whole dome was resplendent with its covering of gilded tiles. The vast concave was plated with burnished silver, and the flower ornaments of the countless *cassettoni* were mirrored with a thousand glittering reflections in the polished pavement of porphyry and ever precious marble. Eight porphyry columns adorned the drum of the dome. In front of the *cella* facing the door was a beautiful aedicule formed by a circle of carayatidae in gilt bronze - each one was a masterpiece of Diogenes of Athens and each contained a statue of Jupiter. The rest of the Pantheon's ornamentation can only be guessed at based on the scraps and relics that have been discovered on site over the centuries.[17]

---

[17] Under Pope Eugenius IV, a head of Agrippa and the metal hoof of a horse were found near the Pantheon; therefore, it has been surmounted that the façade was surmounted by a car and a stature of Agrippa. Vasquez proposes that there was a bas-relief of Jupiter fulminating the giants in the tympanum; statues of Augustus and Agrippa, made of the same metal, would have stood on either side of the portico. A massive porphyry sarcophagus which now adorns the Corsini Chapel of Saint John Lateran and contains the body of Clement XII once stood in the portico of the Pantheon, as did another similar sarcophagus which was sold by the canons and taken to Ferrara. The two granite lions which now stand under the fountain de' termini were also found among the debris of the portico in 1493.

No archaeologist or scholar has been able to determine the dimensions of the Pantheon's forecourt or those of its three-story trabeation. The most important uncertainty of the Pantheon's interior is its problematic attics story. The original ornamental elements of this story - a veneer of decoration - were removed in 1747 for reasons unknown. In 1930, Alberto Terenzio restored a portion of this upper stage in accordance with a drawing left by the Renaissance artist Raphael, and from this drawing and his own archaeological investigations, Terenzio was able to deduce that the original attic story of the Pantheon contained 64 pilasters of polychrome marble framed in porphyry. Raphael's drawing suggests that these pilasters were arranged in sets of four within each of the Pantheon's 16 panels.

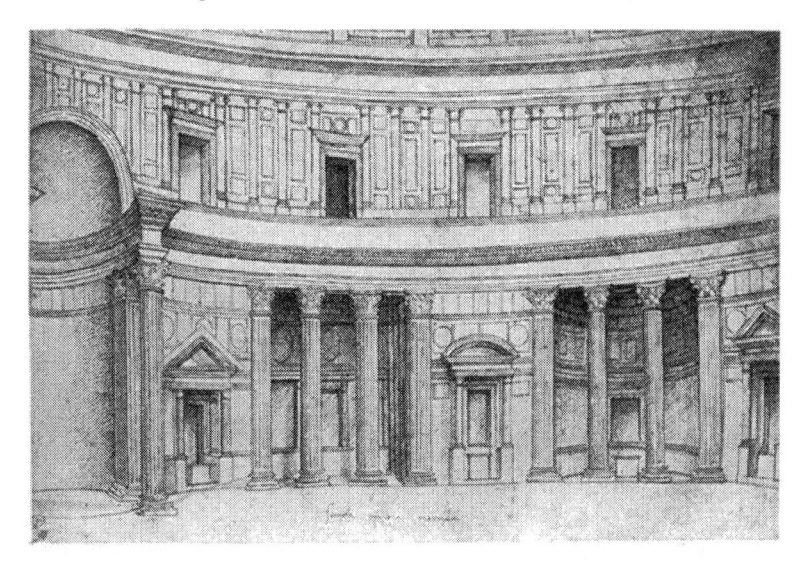

Raphael's drawing of the Pantheon

Many scholars have also speculated that bronze stars were affixed to the center of each of the Pantheon's coffers, while others maintain that these were actually bronze rosettes. In either case, most of these metallic embellishments have either fallen off or were forcibly removed from the coffers. This is hard to see given the many restorations that have been done to the Pantheon's surfaces, but prior to these restorations, however, it was possible to see abundant evidence of their hooks and cramps.

There is also much debate regarding the wide band of concrete that surrounds the oculus about the coffers. Some scholars have suggested that this surface was originally painted, while others believe that its discoloration is in large part due to the effects of moisture. If it was painted, it likely depicted the belt of the zodiac at the point of conjunction between the sun and the moon.

Thus, the Pantheon concealed an ineffably sumptuous interior within an exterior that incorporated the conventional elements of a monumental trabeated pedimented temple front. As the building was situated among civic structures to its east, west, and south, its exterior view was largely traditional with the exception of its most unusual golden dome. Glittering in the rays of the sun, the Pantheon's dome must have provided a stunning focal point for the city, and since it was crowned with glistening golden and bronze structures, the dome of the Pantheon would have made for a most impressive sight.

Chapter 3: The Meaning of Hadrian's Pantheon

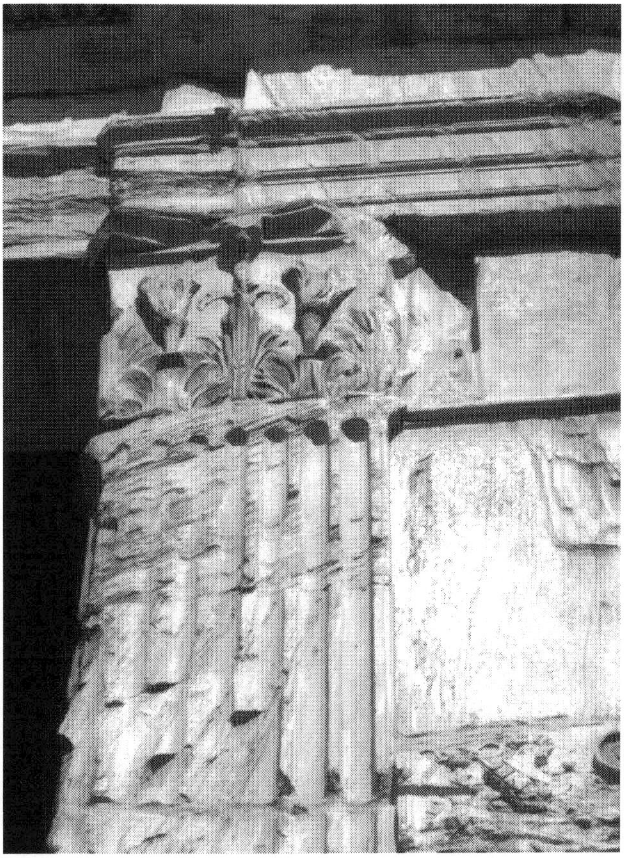

Pictures of carvings on the porch side of the Pantheon

"Perhaps we should surmise that the ancient's devotion to the gods was limitless; perhaps that it was the emperor's self-regard that knew no bounds, and that this sacred-seeming place may, in fact, have been a ruler's tribute to his own Imperial self. We aren't even positive which emperor we should credit, and architects today aren't entirely sure why the dome hasn't collapsed. Nor have they cracked the sublime math of the Pantheon's architect. The Pantheon's interior, subject to ever0shifting light and shadow, is an apt metaphor for all we don't know about the building, and the ancients who conceived it." - Amy Finnerty, *Wall Street Journal* columnist.

Though the Pantheon's structural integrity has been restored, no architect has been able to penetrate the mystery that shrouds its meaning. That said, as the 19th century art historians concluded after their many years spent within the magnificent walls of the Pantheon, "no architect could have been inspired with so sublime a conception when merely meditating the construction of a bath."

While it's safe to assume there was plenty of importance attached to the Pantheon, leading Pantheon scholar William MacDonald has confessed that it will probably never be possible to say with any precision what the Pantheon meant to Hadrian and his contemporaries. But even though the meaning of the Pantheon has been described as both "enigmatic" and "problematic," many scholars have made a number of interesting suggestions. In 1923, Arturo Graf suggested that the Pantheon was dedicated primarily to Saturn; in 1968, Kjeld DeFine Licht proposed that it was a monument to the gens Julia and its divine ancestors; in 1984, Henri Stierlin claimed that it was a solar temple; and in 1989, Giangiacomo Martines was arguing that its cupola was a unique example of ideal geometry.

Clearly, no consensus has ever been reached, but MacDonald has recently argued that the meaning of the extraordinary structure lies (beyond its dedication to the gods) in its role as the temple of Rome and thus of all things Roman.

Indra Kagis McEwen argues that it was not uncommon for Roman emperors to employ architecture as a form of rhetoric, and McEwen claims there are a number of specific reasons that Hadrian's Pantheon should be considered to be a rhetorical structure. It features an unequivocal orientation, as its sequential development displays a measured projection from beginning to middle to end. By McEwen's reading, the Pantheon as designed by Hadrian represents what was, in Roman rhetorical terms, a *quaesito finita*; the building's structure emulated a limited, bounded question which plead for the cause of imperial order. The celestial gods, then, sat as the divine judges before whom Hadrian pled his cause.

Given that Agrippa's first Pantheon was destroyed, restored, and destroyed again within less than a century, McEwen argues that the Romans would have likely believed that the celestial gods had an intense dislike for Agrippa's Pantheon, especially given its hubristic assumptions about the divinity of living emperors. Only the gods had been described as "*augustus*" before Caesar Octavian received this as his honorary praenomen. In fact, just a few years after the original Pantheon was first constructed - before the entire temple was twice destroyed by fire - many of the objects within Agrippa's Pantheon were struck by fire.

Hadrian, like most Romans of his day, may not have considered the fires which plagued the first Pantheon to have been divine in origin, but he would not have doubted that the lightning that had been attacking the structure since its conception in 27 BCE could not have come from anywhere but the heavens. As emperor, Hadrian also would have known that it was his responsibility to maintain the Roman empire as an image of the cosmic order. Under such an interpretation, if the hubris of the original Pantheon had upset that cosmic order, it was up to Hadrian to rebuild the structure in a manner that would be more pleasing to the celestial gods, and the challenge in rebuilding the Pantheon would be to rejoin the Imperial order and its rules of law to the divine order by which it was initiated and subsumed. Thus, Hadrian undertook the *quaesito finita* with the "*causa*" of restoring, and reconciling, the Pantheon.

In this view, it is readily evident that Hadrian would have wanted his project to be understood as a restoration of Agrippa's building in order that his project would seem to vindicate the Imperial order which had been initiated under Augustus (and, by extension, under Agrippa). Hadrian was compelled to prove not only the legitimacy of his own ascension, but also the propriety of the imperial power of Augustus and every emperor who succeeded him.

McEwen suggests that the Pantheon be read as a judicial causa in four parts. First, the forecourt should be read as an exordium, a part of a speech that was meant to prepare the audience in such a way that it would most readily and agreeably hear the rest of the speech. The porch was the narratio, the statement of facts, while the rotunda was the probation, both argument and proof. Finally, the Basilica of Neptune stood as the peroration or conclusion. If so, the Romans must have believed the Pantheon persuaded the gods since the Pantheon was largely unharmed after Hadrian rebuilt it. Indeed, it is arguably the best-preserved building of Roman antiquity.

Most significant to Hadrian's rhetorical plea was the probation, the Pantheon's magnificent domed rotunda. Two scholars of the Roman Pantheon, K. de Fine Licht and William Loerke, have both published drawings of the way in which the cylinder of the rotunda is divided into 16 parts. As Loerke demonstrates, these divisions yield the generating module for the entire building, right down to the size of the oculus. McEwen argues that these 16 parts of the rotunda's cylinder were meant to represent the 16 parts of the sky as set out by the *Etrusca disciplina*;[18] thus, the panels of the Pantheon were meant to represent the sky from where the lightning that had harassed and eventually destroyed the original structure had come.

Of further significance to the meaning of the Pantheon's structure was the reason for the 16 divisions of the Etruscan sky. According to the Roman author Cicero, the Etruscan sky system had 16 sections because it had to do with orientation; the Etruscans arrived at the number 16 by twice doubling the four cardinal points.

Following Stefan Weinstock's catalog of which deities occupied which region of the Etruscan sky, it becomes possible to gain a deeper understanding of many of Hadrian's renovations to the Pantheon, especially his reversal of its orientation. While Agrippa's Pantheon had faced south, Hadrian rotated his structure so that it faced north, the region of beginnings and endings. Of the gods who inhabit the regions of the north, some of the more notable include Jupiter (king of the Roman gods) and Janus (the two-faced god of doorways, beginnings, and endings). As a reflection of the Etruscan sky system, then, the Pantheon's rotunda placed Janus exactly where

---

[18] A systematic collection of Etruscan teachings about how to divine the will of the gods and act in accordance with it. These teachings were especially concerned with the interpretation of thunder and lightning. Repeated references to the ritual founding of cities can also be found within the *disciplina*.

he belongs in the north-facing doorway.

Unfortunately, there is no record of the statues Hadrian placed in the other 15 niches of the Pantheon. However, McEwen has deduced that when Hadrian held court in the Pantheon's rotunda,[19] he sat in the main southern apse facing the doorway. If this holds true, Hadrian must have spoken from the domain of Neptune. When seated in the tribunal in the Pantheon's main apse, Hadrian thus would have become Neptune, the Roman god who ruled the sea as Jupiter's brother and equal, and who was entrusted with bringing back the sun. Following this hypothesis, the measurement of the main apse - 9 meters - must also have been significant, as it precisely matched the width of the oculus, its heavenly counterpart. Just as in the cosmos, Neptune, who ruled the sea, equaled Jupiter, who ruled the sky. This arrangement also seems to have implied that Hadrian ruled the earth just as the gods ruled in the cosmos.

Imperial order, as represented by the Pantheon, was designed to correspond with celestial order, the order of the 16 part sky by which the earth is oriented and given its proper direction. Without the sky, the earth would have no orientation, no center, and no limit; indeed, it would be like the boundless surface of the centerless pavement of the floor in the Pantheon's rotunda. The floor is indeed a sharp contrast to the concentric dome above it, whose circumference at its springing corresponds exactly to the circumference of its cylinder. The cylinder, in turn, establishes the position and size of the floor's peripheral limit. When considered alone, however, the floor is an un-centered expanse of space; like the earth, it is unknown and unknowable beyond its horizon. In the absence of the circular boundary that confines it and brings it to an end, it would surely continue on forever. Indeed, the squares and circles of the Pantheon's rotunda were the geometric symbols of the order and orientation by which Roman cities were traditionally established.[20]

In the Etrusco-Roman tradition, only orientating temples could be round, and since the rotunda of the Pantheon embodied the order of the Etruscan sky by condensing the celestial order into a circular diagram, it was this kind of temple. Thus, the Pantheon may have been, possibly as Hadrian intended, an inaugurator of space and considered the founding temple of the world's foremost Imperial city. As one of Hadrian's first acts upon his return to Rome in 117, he laid the 10,000 metric ton concrete foundation of the Pantheon's rotunda in an unbroken circle buried deep (15 meters) in the ground of the hallowed Campus Martius. In so doing, he laid the

---

[19] "with the assistance of the foremost men…always seated on a tribunal so that whatever was done was made public" (Dio LXIX.7.1)

[20] In order to found a city, an auger would place himself facing (usually) south and sketch a circular diagram—called a *templum*—in two ways. In the first sketch, he circumscribed the required area of the sky; in the second, he drew the same diagram on the ground. His goal was to orient the earth by the sunrise and sunset of the sky. The placement of the augur's sky temple would have had something to do with invoking at least some of the deities. The augur would have given the circular diagram its orientation by quartering it with a cross drawn through it. The square itself was a heavenly sky (*ouranian*) figure that had its corners at the outside rather than at the center; thus, every *templum* was built in the shape of a rectangle, with the notable exception of the inaugural, orientating *templum*, which was circular.

foundations of his empire. By negotiating the release of the recently conquered provinces of Armenia, Assyria, and Mesopotamia, Hadrian also had the permanent and palpable boundaries necessary for a properly founded Imperial city.

There may be further rhetorical significance to be found in Hadrian's retention of the structure's nickname. Like the structure itself, the name "pantheon" would have further promoted the imperial cult. "*Theios*" was a Greek word and the equivalent of the Roman epithet "divus," which was used to signify the divinity of emperors. "Pan" was the Greek word for "all," so the Pantheon thus referred to all such *divi*.

Hadrian, a poet, would have known well that words may carry multiple meanings, so he may have had another reason to retain the name "pantheon." There is another Greek work – *thea* - which refers to the act of looking at and gazing upon, as well as to the place from which that looking takes place. It refers to contemplation and the act of contemplating. "Thea" was closely related to the Latin word "*contemplatio*," which, not incidentally, was the word used in the *Etrusca disciplina* for the temple-drawing, boundary-fixing, city-drawing ritual. Taken in this context, the word "pantheon" would denote a ritual of foundation that occurs "*pante*," or everywhere. With his careful, reconciliatory renovations to the Pantheon, Hadrian was thus reconciling and re-founding the Roman Imperial order with the divine order by which it was both initiated and subsumed.

Christiane L. Joost-Gaugier offers another, complementary reading of the Pantheon's meaning. Joost-Gaugier claims that the structure is a Pythagorean composition that was meant to denote order and beauty. According to Joost-Gaugier, Hadrian decided to erect in the center of the city of Rome, in an area dedicated to the cult of the emperor, not just another temple but the most grand, innovative, and complex secular temple of Roman antiquity. He would have done this in order to convey to the Romans a very carefully crafted and distinct reminder of his divinely ordained imperial power.

Joost-Gaugier stresses that the Pantheon was constructed around a central axis, and this, she argues, as well as its circular plan, its orientation to the four cardinal directs, and the hemispherical character of its dome, are all indicative that it was designed with cosmic and Pythagorean concerns. Since Hadrian was well-versed in arithmetic and passionate about his interest in the Greek East, it is easy to see how he could have turned to Pythagorean sources as he was designing the Pantheon.

Though it is difficult to pin down the precise sources for Hadrian's articulation of the idea of the cosmos, the ingenuity of Pythagorean arithmetic seemingly lurks behind several elements of the Pantheon's design. The rotunda, the central and most important part of the Pantheon's design, is dominated by the number 1, and Pythagoreans considered the number 1 as the "unit" or "monad" due to its indivisible character and the fact that it is the only number perfect in power. To the Pythagoreans, the number 1 has an ineffable nature which represents pure celestial light, and fittingly, the rotunda is the Pantheon's sole source of illumination. The celestial light pours forth into the temple where it spreads out, unimpeded, and rules over everything with divine authority.

Most significantly, the number 1 is the Sun for Pythagoreans.[21] In the Pantheon, the sun and its singularity are represented by the oculus. Given Hadrian's proclivity towards apotheosis, it is not unlikely to suggest that the oculus of the Pantheon was meant to be a hyper-visible symbol of Hadrian himself.[22]

Radiating from the Pantheon's oculus are 28 ribs, which form the planetary vault that reaches down to the supporting cylinder below. The Pythagoreans thought that 28 was the number of the moon, as there were 28 days in a lunar month.

Attached to both the singular oculus and its 28 ribs are the vault's 5 coffered rings. This combination would have been extremely unusual to the ancients, but it makes sense in a Pythagorean context. According to the Pythagorean Theon of Smyrna, the number 5 was the proportional arithmetic mean of the decad and the first fully circular number. Since the number 5 encompasses both the number two (the first even number) and the number three (the first odd number), the Pythagoreans considered it to be both male and female. For this reason, Pythagoreans often considered 5 to be the number of marriage. Thus, the Pantheon's domed rotunda - the height and heart of the structure, around and below which the entire rest of the building is organized - symbolizes the accord of the sun and the moon.

Below the dome is a cylinder which is characterized by 3 large semi-circular niches and four 4 rectangular niches. Together, these form 7 large shrines (*aediculae*) which are well-suited to sculptures. The trigon, 3, is the first of the rectinilinear figures and is both line and surface, so it is the principle of triplicity or the triangle. Indeed, it is a triangle which is formed by these 3 semi-circular niches. This is significant, as the Pythagoreans also considered Apollo to be the apex of a given triangle. The Pythagoreans also considered 3 to be the ideal number since it has a beginning, a middle, and an end. As a result, the number 3 symbolizes totality.

The number 4 was also esteemed by the Pythagoreans, who held the quaternary in high regard because it seemed to outline the entire nature of the universe, especially the four seasons and the four elements. In the Pythagorean cosmology, the numbers 3 and 4 when taken together represent the cosmos. Indeed, this pair of numbers was believed to provide the key to the universe. 3, the mean between two extremes, unfolds into 4, which is the first number to produce

---

[21] Thus Apollo, the sun god, whose name means "free of multiplicity" or "oneness."

[22] There exists a papyrus fragment in which the succession of Hadrian was announced by Apollo himself on the day of Trajan's death. Thus Hadrian may have claimed to have been called and sanctioned by the supreme god of the Pythagorean monad and deified as the early representative of the sun god from the moment of his accession. This announcement corresponded with a prediction made by Aelius Hadrianus, grand uncle of Hadrian and master of astrology. Indeed, it was Aelius Hadrianus who prophesized that his newborn great nephew would one day rule the world.

a solid form.

Their sum, 7, was also revered, as the 7 strings of Pythagoras' lyre were believed to symbolize the order of the cosmos. 7 was both the number of the planets and their modes. 7 was also the symbol of Apollo's birthday. In the Pantheon, the sequence from the monad to the heptad totals 28, the number of the dividing ribs which radiate from the rotunda. The 7 numbers doubled equals 64, and indeed the Pantheon features 64 panels in its intermediate level.

Below the 7 "cosmic" *aediculae* are 8 smaller *aediculae*. According to the Pythagoreans, the number 8 was the symbol of egalitarian justice. Pythagoras himself was believed to have invented the 8th octave when he added an 8th string to his 7-stringed lyre, thus obtaining *harmonia*, equilibrated tuning, balance, and proportion. To the Pythagoreans, the number 8 was "justice," as it is the first number that is able to be divided into two equal numbers that will, when divided again, produce two more equal numbers.

With the aforementioned *aediculae* and the *aediculae* in the entrance opening, the total number of *aediculae* in the Pantheon's rotunda is 16, another number that the Pythagoreans considered ideal. 16 was not only the double octave but also the product of four and the first number with three-dimensional extension. The number 16, as the product of 4 x 4, makes an equilateral and prime cube, and accordingly, it is the only geometric form that has a perimeter which is the same on all four of its sides.

Even the Pantheon's 64 pilasters had Pythagorean significance, as 64, the product of 8 (octaves) x 8 (octaves), was believed by the Pythagoreans to be the greatest unifying number.

To the eyes of a Pythagorean, then, the whole of the pavement of the Pantheon's rotunda is composed exclusively of squares which are inscribed within circles and circles, which are themselves inscribed within squares. The entire circle of the rotunda can be contained within a square, and if the Pantheon was of such an elevation that the hemisphere of the dome were to be continued below so as to be a whole sphere, that sphere would fit into a cube, as its horizontal and vertical axes would be the same.[23] The Pantheon's original attic with its 64 panel must be understood in this light, as 64 is the only number which the Pythagoreans considered to be both circular and a cube.[24] Only in the number 64 could both circle and square be reconciled.

Linking the *pronaos* of the Pantheon to its interior space are the *pronaos*' 16 Corinthian columns. These columns are arranged so that the frontal façade of the Pantheon presents 8 columns, thereby suggesting a link between the structure's sacred and judicial functions. The

---

[23] The squaring of a circle was one of the greatest mysteries of Pythagorean arithmetic; therefore, this came to be a goal for many Pythagorean practitioners.

[24] A circular number is a number whose power ends in the same digit. In this case, the number four has a cube of sixty-four, which ends with the number four. Sixty-four also represents the "cubic solid" of the number four, as its first square is also a cube.

other 8 columns of the Pantheon's *pronaos* are arranged in a 2 x 2 = 4 = 2 + 2 = 4 arrangement on either side of the entrance passage way. Since these equations total 8, they suggest—in Pythagorean terms—the equality and balance of the law. In nearly all of its elements, the Pantheon thus seems to have been designed with perfect numbers in mind.

In the view of Anatolius, an early Roman scholar of Pythagorean philosophy, 16 was the perfect number because 16 is the only number whose area is equal to its perimeter as the product of 4 x 4. Thus the (2 x 2) + (2 + 2) = 8 formation by which the columns of the pronaos are arranged, is uniformly even. Another element of 16's alleged perfection is that it is the sum of the dividers of the number 12, which was the Pythagorean perfect "super number." 16 is dependent on doubling the properties of the number 8, security, harmony, and justice. The number 16 also appears within the Pantheon's interior, in the articulation of the circle of the Pantheon's plan. Above this circle are the 28 coffers, and 28 was another number which Anatolius considered to be perfect.[25]

Given the abundant archaeological evidence of Pythagorean design throughout the entire Pantheon, not to mention Hadrian's known affiliation with the Pythagoreans, it's not a stretch to believe that the Pantheon was constructed by Hadrian with a uniquely Pythagorean cosmological language in mind.

Taken together, these elements of Pythagorean cosmology, which are found in abundance within the Pantheon's design, suggest that Pantheon was built as a symbol of the imperial prophecy that accompanied his birth. In essence, the Pantheon signified the conjunction of the sun and the new moon, as well as Hadrian's destiny to rule the Roman world. As Hadrian's imperial authority was established by Apollo—Hadrian's divine father and protector—Hadrian was able to legitimize his reign as a sovereign god in even a daunting Roman political climate, which by then was growing more skeptical by the day, by building a great monument for Apollo and the other 11 main gods of the Roman pantheon. The structure was a tangible manifestation of Hadrian's all-consuming ambition and a representation of the reputation of himself that he wanted to project to Rome.

Hadrian, like all educated men of his day, knew that perfect numbers denoted divine presences, and he cleverly employed this knowledge in the construction of his temple, a tactic that made the Pantheon far more effective as a piece of imperial propaganda than any singular sculpture could ever have hoped to be. When Hadrian sat in judgment in the apse of the Pantheon at the apex of the triangle, he transformed into Apollo himself. The spectacular golden temple, with its radiant golden dome that could be seen throughout all of Rome, naturally bestowed a sense of divine authority as well, and the Pantheon thus guaranteed Hadrian's solar immortality as the king of the universe. With concrete evidence, the Pantheon made the bold claim that

---

[25] Because of the dependency of the number twenty-eight on the number four. The four weeks of the moon times its seven phases equals twenty-eight.

regardless of the Senate's opinion, Hadrian would be a god after he died, as he had been a god from the very day he was born.

Chapter 4: The Pantheon after Hadrian

A modern picture of the interior

Stefan Bauer's picture of the interior

"When friends come to Rome in early summer to visit me I like to take them to the Pantheon during thunderstorms and stand them beneath the opening of the feathery, perfectly proportioned dome as rain falls through the open roof against the marble floor and lightning scissors through the wild and roiled skies. The emperor Hadrian rebuilt the temple to honor gods no longer worshiped, but you can feel the brute passion in that ardor in the Pantheon's grand and harmonious shape. I think gods have rarely been worshiped so well." - Pat Conroy, a *New York Times* bestselling author

Only one Roman emperor after Hadrian dared to make even the most minor renovations to the Pantheon's sublime structure. In 202, at the command of the emperor Severus, rectangular indentations were cut into the Pantheon's ceiling and decorated with bronze rosettes and molding. An inscription on the lower cornice of the Pantheon reports this reparation was made under the emperor Severus in 202. A tablet which may be seen during the descent from the Pantheon's upper level describes how the emperor Severus escaped from an incursion of the Gauls on the city. According to this tablet, while Severus was escaping, he overtook in the Via Aurelia a party of vestal virgins trying to make their way to a place of safety. He immediately stopped them and placed them in his chariot, and he did not leave them until he had deposited them in security at Ceri, though at some point along the way it obliged him to leave his own wife and children in peril."

An ancient bust of Severus

As the Roman Empire began to collapse, the Pantheon was slowly dismantled. Its massive bronze doors were carried off by Genseric in 455, and the gilt bronze covering of the dome was removed by Constantius III in the early 5th century. This covering was carried to Sicily and was ultimately intended to be taken to Constantinople along with a number of other Roman spoils, but Constantius III was assassinated in 421 and the dome covering was intercepted by the Saracens.

In 397, the emperor Honorius had issued a decree ordering all of the old temples in the Roman Empire to be closed, so the Pantheon basically went unused for at least two centuries until Saint Augustine finally proposed that the old pagan temples should be turned into Christian temples rather than be completely destroyed. Pope Gregory I acceded, so on May 13th, 610, the Pantheon was reopened under the dedication of Sainta Maria and Martyres in memory of the great number of bones of martyrs who were then brought there for burial. The dedication, however, was to "All Saints," carrying out the sublime idea of completeness that marked the temple's original dedication. Boniface IV consecrated the structure *"cunctis sanctis"* (to all things sacred).

In the 12th century, Whit Sunday was celebrated with special honor in the Pantheon. The Pope himself sang the office and pronounced a homily. A ceremony of showering roses down the oculus in special commemoration of the descent of the Holy Spirit upon the whole church ensued.

When the Popes removed the seat of government to Avignon, the Pantheon was subjected to greater havoc than it had ever experienced in its already tumultuous history. The city fell prey to a number of rival families, each of whom established themselves in some building which, given the strength of its construction, could be easily defended (including the Coliseum and the Mausoleum of Hadrian among others). Eventually, the Pantheon became the stronghold of the Crescenzi family. It was considered a great spot for withstanding a siege, especially with its 19 foot tall windowless walls. While the Crescenzi family expected the Pantheon to protect them, they were not concerned about protecting the Pantheon, and during their occupancy it was terribly shattered and encumbered with ruins.

In the 50 years following their return to Rome, the Popes were preoccupied with re-establishing their supremacy over these contending factions, and Pope Martin V (1417-1431) was concerned with putting his city in order. Pope Martin V revived the College of Aediles and entrusted them with the care of public buildings, but he took it upon himself to tend to the Pantheon. He removed the sheds and low shops which the Crescenzi had built under the protection of the Pantheon's portico, reinstated its pillars, polished its marble, and repaired its dome, which had been so shaken by earthquakes that it would require further renovations under Eugenius IV in 1437. The successor of Eugenius IV, Nicholas V, then covered the dome with lead in the hopes that this would prevent the dome from sustaining such extensive damage in subsequent earthquakes. Pope Pius IV (1559-1566) installed a massive new set of doors 16" thick and made of bronze-plated oak, and Clement IX (1567-1570) subsequently studded these doors with large nails.

Martin V

Pictures of the portico

The papal renovations were halted briefly due to Pope Urban VIII's ardent desire to complete Saint Peter's in the first half of the 17th century. Pope Urban took the bronze beams from the portico of the Pantheon for use in the baldachino of the high altar in Saint Peter's,[26] as it was alleged that the woodwork on which the beams rested was old and would soon be unable to sustain the weight of the beams, which was said to have amount to 44,000,250 Roman pounds. A few decades later, Pope Alexander VII (1655-1667) completed the reinstatement of the Pantheon's portico by supplying two of its former columns which he had discovered in the neighborhood of S. Luigi dei Francesi nearly 100 yards from the site of the Pantheon. The columns were each monoliths of granite, standing 38 feet 6 inches tall with a circumference of 14 feet. That they had managed to become separated from the site of the Pantheon by a distance of almost 100 yards is a testament to the fury of devastation the Pantheon had withstood over the past several centuries.

Pope Benedict XIV (1740-1758) commissioned Fea to clear out the base of the building on the

---

[26] Ironically, the 440,887 pounds of beams and 9,374 pounds of nails in the apostolic foundry were mixed so copiously with gold and silver that they proved unsatisfactory for artillery.

east, and he declared that henceforth the building should always be kept in repair at the expense of the Palazzo Apostolico. Benedict XIV considered building a lantern over the Pantheon's oculus, but he did not have time to accomplish this before his death. Pius IX continued the renovations begun by Benedict XIV, including laying bare the entire depth of the walls (10 feet in total) and devoting some of the finest blocks of precious marbles to the restoration of the Pantheon's worn pavement.

The Pantheon has also rendered a great number of services to the arts. In 1543, one of the Pantheon's canons, Don Desiderio, brought forth a quantity of earth from various holy places in the East and established the foundations of a chapel which he had restored within the Pantheon. It was in this chapel that Desiderio instituted a society of artists - painters, sculptors, architects, engravers, and all other "creators of beautiful art" - under the title of "S. Giuseppe di Terra Santa."

In 1833, S. Giuseppe di Terra Santa exhumed and verified the remains of Raphael, which they then re-interred within the Pantheon. The event was memorialized with a tablet inscribed with a quote by Cardinal Bembow: "*Postquam oculis nostris carissima vidimus ossa, Carius haud usquam quod videamus erit*" ("After our eyes beheld these bones, hardly ever again would we see anything more precious"). It had been the dying wish of the great painter to be interred in the sublime receptacle of the Pantheon; Raphael himself designated the spot for his sepulture and expressed his desire for an altar and a statue of the Virgin Mary to be erected there. Lorenzetto fulfilled his last wishes, and Winkelman pronounced the statue of the Virgin to be the best specimen of modern sculpture. Carlo Maratti also established a bust for Raphael there in 1674 as a testimony of his gratitude for the benefit he had derived from studying Raphael's works. Next to the bones of the Renaissance master lie the remains of his betrothed, Maria, who only survived him by three months.

Raphael

A picture of Raphael's tomb

In stating (and accomplishing) his desire of resting beneath the dome of the Pantheon, Raphael started something of a trend, as a number of other artists and distinguished men crowded in to lay their ashes beside his own.[27] So numerous were these memorials that by the beginning of the 19th century, they threatened to convert Sta. Maria ad Martyres into a Hall of Busts. By 1820, Canova had received an order to remove these busts from the Pantheon and arrange them instead in the lower rooms of the Capitol.

---

[27] Among these were Baldassare Peruzzi, Pierino del Vaga, Giovanni da Udine, Taddeo Zuccari, Annibale Caracci, Nicolas Poussin, Raphael Mengs, Flaminio Vacc, the sculptor, Winkelman, Metastasio the poet, Cimarosa, the composer, and Cardinal Gonsalvi, who was a minister and faithful friend of Pius VII.

During the late 19th century, a number of important archaeological excavations were undertaken at the Pantheon, and during the course of these excavations, the interior pavement was restored. As a result of these excavations and renovations, the Pantheon's original materials, including gigantic cuttings of porphyry, pavonazzetto, giallo antico, and granite, were preserved, as were the structure's original designs. Despite serious losses to the exterior and interior ornamentation that had served only to embellish the Pantheon's ornamentation, the Pantheon today survives almost entirely intact as it was conceived and constructed by Hadrian.

A 19th century painting of the Pantheon

From roughly the 7th century, architects have attempted to model their own creations upon the Pantheon, yet none of their efforts have ever been able to surpass the Pantheon itself. Not even the sublime Saint Peter's Basilica can even begin to approach the splendor of the Pantheon. There is no building that can match the Pantheon's sense of simple, unobtrusive grandeur or create the same reflection of an all-surrounding, all-pervading providence. While the Pantheon has for countless centuries afforded a beautiful model to direct and purify the imaginations of architects across countless countries, it seems almost as if the same kind of special providence by which the structure itself is characterized has kept it from being vulgarized by an onslaught of countless replications. Of all the many architects who have sought to imitate the Pantheon, not one has actually been able to accomplish any kind of a true reproduction of its structure.

Seen at any season, and by any light, the Pantheon stands unmatched in its grandeur and majesty. Though Hadrian's intentions behind the Pantheon's design remain an enigma, it is nevertheless obvious that the construction of his building is not only a rare triumph but an example of sublime art.

Clayton Tang's picture of the Pantheon

Online Resources

Other books about Ancient Rome by Charles River Editors

Other books about the Punic Wars on Amazon

Bibliography

Books about the Pantheon

Claridge, Amanda (1998). Rome. Oxford Archaeological Guides. Oxford Oxfordshire: Oxford University Press. ISBN 0-19-288003-9.

Cowan, Henry (1977). The Master Builders: : A History of Structural and Environmental Design From Ancient Egypt to the Nineteenth Century. New York: John Wiley and Sons. ISBN 0-471-02740-5.

Favro, Diane (2005). "Making Rome a World City". The Cambridge Companion to the Age of Augustus. Cambridge University Press. pp. 234–263. ISBN 978-0-521-00393-3.

Hetland, L. M. (2007). Dating the Pantheon. Journal of Roman Archaeology 20 (1). pp. 95–112. ISSN 1047-7594.

King, Ross (2000). Brunelleschi's Dome. London: Chatto & Windus. ISBN 0-7011-6903-6.

Kleiner, Fred S. (2007). A History of Roman Art. Belmont: Wadsworth Publishing. ISBN 0-534-63846-5.

Lancaster, Lynne C. (2005). Concrete Vaulted Construction in Imperial Rome: Innovations in Context. Cambridge: Cambridge University Press. ISBN 0-521-84202-6.

Loewenstein, Karl (1973). The Governance of Rome. The Hague, Netherlands: Martinus Nijhof. ISBN 978-90-247-1458-2.

MacDonald, William L. (1976). The Pantheon: Design, Meaning, and Progeny. Cambridge, MA: Harvard University Press. ISBN 0-674-01019-1.

Marder, Tod A. (1980). Specchi's High Altar for the Pantheon and the Statues by Cametti and Moderati. The Burlington Magazine 122 (922) (The Burlington Magazine Publications, Ltd.). pp. 30–40. JSTOR 879867.

Marder, Tod A. (1991). Alexander VII, Bernini, and the Urban Setting of the Pantheon in the Seventeenth Century. The Journal of the Society of Architectural Historians 50 (3) (Society of Architectural Historians). pp. 273–292. doi:10.2307/990615. JSTOR 990615.

Mark, R.; Hutchinson, P. (1986). On the structure of the Pantheon. Art Bulletin 68 (1) (College Art Association). pp. 24–34. doi:10.2307/3050861. JSTOR 3050861.

Ramage, Nancy H.; Ramage, Andrew (2009). Roman art : Romulus to Constantine (5th ed.). Upper Saddle River, N.J.: Pearson Prentice Hall. ISBN 978-0-13-600097-6.

Roth, Leland M. (1992). Understanding Architecture: Its Elements, History, And Meaning. Boulder: Westview Press. ISBN 0-06-438493-4.

Thomas, Edmund (1997). The Architectural History of the Pantheon from Agrippa to Septimius Severus via Hadrian. Hephaistos 15. pp. 163–186.

Wilson-Jones, Mark (2003). Principles of Roman Architecture. New Haven: Yale University Press. ISBN 0-300-10202-X.

Articles on the Pantheon

"A Curious Description of the Pantheon at Rome, in a Letter from a Gentleman, after Just Visiting It, to His Friend." The Weekly Amusement. Sept. 1, 1764, pp. 589-590.

Busk, R. H. "The Pantheon." Art-Journal. Issue 83 (Nov. 1868), pp. 233-236.

de Grummond, N. T. 2012. Etrusca disciplina. The Encyclopedia of Ancient History.

Finnerty, Amy. "Masterpiece: Elegant Mystery; That Rome's Pantheon Eludes Historical Certitudes Adds to Its Enduring Magnetism." Wall Street Journal. Jan. 20, 2007, p. 16.

Hölkeskamp, Karl J. "History and Collective Memory in the Middle Republic." A Companion to the Roman Republic. Wiley-Blackwell. West Sussex: 2010.

Joost-Gaugier, Christiane L. "The Iconography of Sacred Space: A Suggested Reading of the Meaning of the Roman Pantheon." Artibus et Historia, Vol. 19, No. 38 (1998) pp. 21-42.

Mark, Robert and Hutchinson, Paul. "On the Structure of the Roman Pantheon." The Art Bulletin, Vol. 68, No. 1 (Mar., 1986), pp. 24-34.

MacDonald, William L. The Pantheon: Design, Meaning, and Progeny. Harvard University Press. Cambridge: 1976.

McEwen, Indra K. "Hadrian's Rhetoric I: The Pantheon." RES: Anthropology and Aesthetics, No. 24 (Autumn, 1993) pp. 55-66.

Swetnam-Burland, M. 2012. Pantheon, Rome. The Encyclopedia of Ancient History.

Wiley, H.W. "The Effect of Fire on Granite." The Classical Weekly. Vol. XIV, No. 16 (1923) p. 128.

Printed in Great Britain
by Amazon